The ACRE Formula© for CRE brokers

INTRODUCTION

In real estate, success hinges on whether your property or service is perceived as the solution to your client's problem. Listings are secured, leases are assigned, and sales are closed only when the client sees a clear fit between their needs and what you offer.

If your offering is the right match, there are only a few core reasons a client might still fail to move forward. While these reasons can be expressed in many ways, they nearly always trace back to one of three root causes. Recognize these causes, respond effectively, and you'll rarely lose a qualified prospect.

Let's be clear: when presented with the ideal property or service, a client has only two choices:

1. **Accept it outright**, or

2. **Accept it with conditions** by:

    o   raising a concern

    o   expressing a frustration, or

    o   stating a position

While unconditional acceptance is ideal, your true value as a real estate professional is showcased when you navigate these conditional roadblocks and still earn the client's commitment.

This book introduces you to **28 things clients say** when they're hesitating over a listing, lease, purchase, or sale — and, more importantly, shows you how to respond.

You'll learn the **ACRE Formula©**, a proven, non-defensive communication strategy that overcomes all 28 deal-breaking scenarios and turns indecision into action.

Potential Real Estate Deal Breakers

"You can't shake hands with a clenched fist." – *Mahatma Gandhi*

Even when the right property or service solution is on the table, a deal can still collapse. Why? Because every stalled or failed transaction boils down to just **three core stress factors**:

1. **Mental Stress**

2. **Emotional Stress**

3. **Positional Stress**

Let's unpack each one.

MENTAL STRESS

Mental stress happens when a client's **fear of taking action outweighs their desire** for your property or service.

If you've ever had a qualified buyer, tenant, or seller suddenly get cold feet—unable to justify the decision despite earlier enthusiasm—that's mental stress at work. Deals die not because the property is wrong, but because fear won the day.

Whose job is it to recognize and resolve mental stress?
Yours. It's *why you get paid.*

In PART 1 of this book, you'll learn exactly what mentally stressed clients say when fear takes over—and you'll get a proven strategy to help them move past it with confidence.

EMOTIONAL STRESS

Emotional stress occurs when a client becomes **frustrated, anxious, resentful, or hostile** during a negotiation.

If you've ever had someone throw up their hands in exasperation and walk away from the table—that's emotional stress shutting the deal down.

Whose role is it to manage the emotional climate?
Yours. Again—*it's why you get paid.*

In PART 2, you'll uncover the phrases emotionally stressed clients use, and you'll master a response strategy that defuses tension, restores calm, and keeps negotiations on track.

POSITIONAL STRESS

Positional stress sets in when two parties **dig in over price, terms, dates, or conditions**—and no one is willing to budge.

If a buyer refuses to meet a seller's fixed price, or a tenant won't match a landlord's requirements, you've got positional stress. Once lines are drawn in the sand, both sides tend to get entrenched—unless you intervene skillfully.

Whose role is it to break the deadlock?
Yours. You guessed it—it's *why you get paid.*

In PART 3, you'll discover the language of positional stress and learn a negotiation method that turns stand-offs into signed agreements.

The better you are at identifying and resolving these three stress factors, the more listings you'll win, the more leases you'll secure, and the more transactions you'll close. That means higher income, a stronger professional brand, and greater time efficiency.

THE JAWS OF DEFENSE

"Speak when you're angry and you'll make the best speech you will ever regret." – *Anonymous*

When clients get stressed, most agents respond on instinct, not strategy. And that instinct often takes the form of one of **four defensive habits** I call the **JAWS of Defense©**:

- **J** – *Justify*

- **A** – *Accuse*

- **W** – *Withdraw*

- **S** – *Sarcasm*

Here's how each one shows up—and why they kill deals:

Justify – Explaining Instead of Resolving

Justification means rationalizing your actions or circumstances instead of addressing the stress.

Examples:

- "Well, I did that because…"

- "That's not what I meant."

- "There was no way to anticipate this."

- "That's how we've always done it."

- "I'm not the one who makes these decisions."

Accuse – Shifting the Blame

Accusation puts the spotlight (and the blame) on someone else.

Examples:

- "Perhaps you should have been clearer in your request."

- "If your secretary had sent the documents earlier, this wouldn't have happened."

- "If you'd been more flexible, the deal might have worked."

Withdraw – Walking Away

Withdrawal means emotionally — or literally — checking out of the negotiation.

Examples:

- "If you're not coming up in price, you'll lose this deal."

- "Call me when you're ready to make a serious offer."

- "If you won't lower your price, we might as well pull the listing."

Sarcasm – Humor With a Sting

Sarcasm disguises irritation as humor, but it only inflames stress.

Examples:

—

- "If you pay peanuts, you get monkeys."

- "I'm not running a charity here!"

- "If I had a dollar for every time I've heard that…"

None of these responses resolve the client's stress.
They *amplify* it.
So, ask yourself: When a client is under pressure, do you instinctively **Justify**, **Accuse**, **Withdraw**, or use **Sarcasm**?

No shame if you do—it's human nature to defend ourselves. But in real estate, instinctive defense costs deals. The key is to replace those JAWS responses with a **non-defensive strategy** that defuses stress and gets the relationship back on track.

That's where the **ACRE Formula**© comes in.

THE ACRE FORMULA ©

"You can't shake hands with a clenched fist." – *Mahatma Gandhi*

Stress is part of every real estate transaction. Buyers and tenants worry about overpaying, uncertain futures, or unexpected financial burdens. Sellers and landlords worry about selling below market, tax implications, or economic pressures.

The **constant** in these scenarios is stress.
The **variable** is how you respond.

When a client is stressed, you have two choices:

- **Defensive** – push back, justify, or blame.

- **Non-defensive** – stay calm, listen, and collaborate.

In a relationship-driven business, the non-defensive approach is the only one that works—and the fastest way to get there is with the **ACRE Formula©**:

- **A** – *Align*

- **C** – *Clarify*

- **R** – *Respond*

- **E** – *Encourage*

Step 1: Align

Alignment is about standing *with* your client, not across from them. It's agreement, acknowledgment, or empathy.

Examples:

- "That's a valid point." (agreement)

- "I can see you feel strongly about this." (acknowledgment)

- "I understand your frustration with the delay. I'd be upset too." (empathy)

Alignment takes the tension down and opens the door to real dialogue.

Step 2: Clarify

Clarifying means uncovering the *root cause* of the stress through thoughtful questions.

A statement like "That's my final offer!" could be:

- Mental stress (fear of overpaying)

- Emotional stress (resentment toward the other party)

- Positional stress (financial limitations or unwillingness to budge)

Examples of clarifying questions:

"May I ask why?"

"What does a solution look like from your perspective?"

"What are you hoping to accomplish?"

Sometimes, the true cause is buried a few layers deep— keep asking until you find it.

Step 3: Respond

Once you know the cause, tailor your response:

3. **Mental stress?** Provide evidence, an action plan, or a guarantee to reduce fear.

4. **Emotional stress?** Offer an apology, explanation, or assurance to lower the emotional temperature.

5. **Positional stress?** Propose a collaborative solution that meets the core needs of both parties.

Step 4: Encourage

Encouragement means affirming progress, confidence, and possibility. It's the bridge from problem-solving to commitment.

Examples:

4. "We're closer than you think to making this work."

5. "I know we can get this across the finish line."

6. "You've made a smart move by getting this far — let's finish strong."

When you replace the **JAWS** of Defense© with the **ACRE** Formula©, you take control of the conversation, keep deals alive, and turn stressed prospects into satisfied clients — without confrontation or lost trust.

PART 1 - Mental Stress

Accelerate successful client engagement experiences by recognizing and resolving your client's fears.

"Mental stress is the condition that exists when a client's fears of taking action become greater than their desire for your property or service offering."

Gerald G. Clerx

MENTAL STRESS

Think back over your real estate career.
How many times have you heard a client respond to your proposal with:

- *"Leave it with me."*

- *"Let me think it over."*

- *"I'll call you when I'm ready to decide."*

What they're really saying is: **you haven't fully eliminated their anxiety about moving forward.**

When mental stress takes hold, the transaction stalls—and it won't regain momentum until the client's underlying fears are recognized and resolved.

Where Mental Stress Comes From

This type of stress can often be traced back to concerns about:

- **Cost** – "The price of the property seems a little aggressive."

- **Capability** – "Frankly, you look young."

- **Capacity** – "I'm not sure now is the right time to buy."

- **Conflict of Interest** – "Isn't it a conflict if the seller pays the fees?"

- **Commitment** – "I just want to talk it over with my partner."

- **Competition** – "You have a lot of competing listings right now."

Whether the client is a buyer, tenant, seller, or landlord, every statement of mental stress hides a **core concern** — and until you identify and address it, the deal is in jeopardy.

How to Alleviate Mental Stress

Once you uncover the true concern, there are only three effective ways to remove it:

1. **Provide Evidence**
   Use facts, case studies, or testimonials to reduce uncertainty.

   - *Statistics* – market data, pricing trends, absorption rates.

   - *Case Studies* – success stories from similar transactions.

   - *Testimonials* – endorsements from past clients.

2. **Recommend an Action Plan**
   Suggest clear steps to resolve the concern — either actions you will take or actions the client can take.

   - Example: "Let's commission an independent appraisal before proceeding."

3. **Offer a Performance Guarantee**
   Give the client a promise of a specific outcome, with no risk to them.

    o   Example: "If we don't secure a signed offer within 30 days, I'll cover the cost of professional staging."

With this in mind, we'll now put the **ACRE Formula©** to the test in handling client objections rooted in mental stress.

First, you'll see the instinctive, defensive reactions (**JAWS of Defense©**).

Then, you'll see the strategic, non-defensive responses using the **ACRE Formula©** — and why they work.

Statements of *Mental* Stress
~ Buyer/Tenant ~

Client Objection

The price of the property seems a little aggressive!

Don't REACT to it ...

An unskilled real estate agent would likely react using one of the following **JAWS** responses:

J ustify ... the circumstances:

Agent: It's in line with the current market.

A ccuse ... the client, or third party, of a wrongdoing:

(unlikely response)

W ithdraw ... from the relationship or situation:

Agent: We can always look at something else.

S arcasm ... directed toward the situation or individual:

Agent: 'A little aggressive' is a bit of an understatement.

Defensive responses such as these will do nothing to alleviate the client's underlying concern. As a result, the client will likely disengage.

Client Objection

The price of the property seems a little aggressive!

'ACRE' it!

A skilled agent would recognize this as a statement of mental stress and respond using the **ACRE** Formula©:

A lign ... **by acknowledging, agreeing or empathizing:**

> Agent: I understand it may seem a little on the high side!

C larify ... **the underlying root cause of the stress:**

> Agent: What specific properties you're comparing this one with?
>> Client: *The last two we looked at!*

R espond ... **with evidence, an action plan or performance guarantee:**

> Agent: Yes, it's true that property values in this part of town are 20% higher than the previous neighborhoods. Here are some of the reasons why this area commands a higher price ... (introduce evidence).

E ncourage ... **the client to move forward:**

> Agent: Does that help to justify the price gap?
>> If 'Yes': Then I recommend we ... (next step).
>> If 'No': Then what would set your mind at ease?

Client Objection

I'm not sure now is the right time to buy.

Don't REACT to it ...

An unskilled real estate agent would likely react using one of the following **JAWS** responses:

J ustify ... the circumstances:

Agent: Historically, the acquisition of real estate has always been a prudent long-term investment strategy.

A ccuse ... the client, or third party, of a wrongdoing:

(unlikely response)

W ithdraw ... from the relationship or situation:

Agent: We can hold off until the market stabalizes.

S arcasm ... directed toward the situation or individual:

Agent: There's no such thing as the wrong time to buy real estate.

Defensive responses such as these will do nothing to alleviate the client's underlying concern. As a result, the client will likely disengage.

Client Objection

I'm not sure now is the right time to buy.

'ACRE' it!

A skilled agent would recognize this as a statement of mental stress and respond using the **ACRE** Formula©:

A lign ... by acknowledging, agreeing or empathizing:

Agent: Timing IS an important consideration when acquiring real estate!

C larify ... the underlying root cause of the stress:

Agent: Why are you feeling uncertain at this time?
   Client: *I've been told the market is due for a major correction.*

Agent: Where did you hear that?
   Client: *A friend of mine in the financial sector said the 'bubble is about to burst.'*

R espond ... with evidence, an action plan or performance guarantee:

Agent: Your friend might be right ... nobody knows for sure. Here's what I recommend we do to mitigate that risk moving forward ... (introduce action plan)?

E ncourage ... the client to move forward:

Agent: Does that seem like a reasonable course of action to take?
   If 'Yes': Then I recommend we ... (next step).
   If '*No*': Then how would you like to proceed?

Client Objection

Isn't it a conflict of interest if the seller/landlord pays the fees?

Don't REACT to it ...

An unskilled real estate agent would likely react using one of the following **JAWS** responses:

J ustify ... the circumstances:

> Agent: I wouldn't be concerned. It's the way we've always done it.

A ccuse ... the client, or third party, of a wrongdoing:

> (unlikely response)

W ithdraw ... from the relationship or situation:

> (unlikely response)

S arcasm ... directed toward the situation or individual:

> Agent: If you'd like ... YOU can pay me as well!

Defensive responses such as these will do nothing to alleviate the client's underlying concern. As a result, the client will likely disengage.

Client Objection

Isn't it a conflict of interest if the seller/landlord pays the fees?

'ACRE' it!

A skilled agent would recognize this as a statement of mental stress and respond using the **ACRE** Formula©:

A lign ... by acknowledging, agreeing or empathizing:

Agent: I can understand why you might think so!

C larify ... the underlying root cause of the stress:

Agent: Are you concerned that I might not represent your best interests in the transaction?

> Client: *It seems to me that it's in your best interest to get a higher price for the seller/landlord.*

R espond ... with evidence, an action plan or performance guarantee:

Agent: Both legally and morally, my fiduciary responsibility is to protect your interests. Real estate agents are governed by Agency law, which eliminates the potential for conflicts of interest.

E ncourage ... the client to move forward:

Agent: Does that help to alleviate your concern?
> If 'Yes': Then let's ... (introduce next step).
> If *'No'*: Then what would set your mind at ease?

Client Objection

I just want to talk it over with my partner.

Don't REACT to it …

An unskilled real estate agent would likely react using one of the following **JAWS** responses:

J ustify … the circumstances:

Agent: The market is quite active. You risk losing this property.

A ccuse … the client, or third party, of a wrongdoing:

(unlikely response)

W ithdraw … from the relationship or situation:

(unlikely response)

S arcasm … directed toward the situation or individual:

Agent: What's to talk about? This is a great deal!

Defensive responses such as these will do nothing to alleviate the client's underlying concern. As a result, the client will likely disengage.

Client Objection

I just want to talk it over with my partner.

'ACRE' it!

A skilled agent would recognize this as a statement of mental stress and respond using the **ACRE** Formula©:

A lign ... by acknowledging, agreeing or empathizing:

Agent: A second opinion is always a good idea.

C larify ... the underlying root cause of the stress:

Agent: Do you anticipate any concerns from your partner?
> Client: *I know price is going to be an issue.*

Agent: Why do you say that?
> Client: *Because she's a CPA and cost containment is what drives all her decisions.*

R espond ... with evidence, an action plan or performance guarantee:

Agent: Then I'd like to propose the three of us get together so I can walk you through all your options. This will ensure we make the best financial decision moving forward.

E ncourage ... the client to move forward:

Agent: How does that sound?
> If 'Yes': Then let's … (introduce next step).
> If '*No*': Then what would you recommend?

Statements of *Mental* Stress

~ Seller/Landlord ~

Client Objection

Your fee seems a little steep.

Don't REACT to it ...

An unskilled real estate agent would likely react using one of the following **JAWS** responses:

J ustify ... the circumstances:

Agent: It's a fairly standard fee amongst real estate service providers.

A ccuse ... the client, or third party, of a wrongdoing:

(unlikely response)

W ithdraw ... from the relationship or situation:

(unlikely response)

S arcasm ... directed toward the situation or individual:

Agent: You know what they say ... if you pay peanuts, you'll end up with monkeys.

Defensive responses such as these will do nothing to alleviate the client's underlying concern. As a result, the client will likely disengage.

Client Objection

Your fee seems a little steep.

'ACRE' it!

A skilled agent would recognize this as a statement of mental stress and respond using the **ACRE** Formula©:

A lign ... by acknowledging, agreeing or empathizing:

Agent: I understand it might seem like a lot of money.

C larify ... the underlying root cause of the stress:

Agent: When you say 'steep' may I ask what you are comparing it with?
> Client: *Company 'X' charges 30% less than you!*

Agent: If I could justify the fee difference between our two companies would that set your mind at ease?
> Client: *It would help.*

R espond ... with evidence, action plan or performance guarantee:

Agent: The primary differences between our two companies is ... (introduce evidence).

E ncourage ... the client to move forward:

Agent: Can you see how this would more than justify the difference in fee structures?
> If *'Yes'*: Then let's ... (introduce next step).
> If *'No'*: Then what would put your mind at ease?

Client Objection

Frankly you look young.

Don't REACT to it ...

An unskilled real estate agent would likely react using one of the following **JAWS** responses:

J ustify ... the circumstances:

Agent: What I lack in experience I more than make up for in enthusiasm and effort.

A ccuse ... the client, or third party, of a wrongdoing:

(unlikely response)

W ithdraw ... from the relationship or situation:

(unlikely response)

S arcasm ... directed toward the situation or individual:

Agent: Thanks ... I moisturize daily!

Defensive responses such as these will do nothing to alleviate the client's underlying concern. As a result, the client will likely disengage.

Client Objection

Frankly you look young.

'ACRE' it!

A skilled agent would recognize this as a statement of mental stress and respond using the **ACRE** Formula©:

A lign ... by acknowledging, agreeing or empathizing:

Agent: You are not the first person to make that observation.

C larify ... the underlying root cause of the stress:

Agent: Sounds to me like you have a concern. May I ask what it is?
> Client: *Your experience level is a bit of a concern.*

R espond ... with evidence, an action plan or performance guarantee:

Agent: I understand. To put your mind at ease can I walk you through a list of other similar projects my team and I have worked on over the past few months … (introduce evidence).

E ncourage ... the client to move forward:

Agent: Does that help to alleviate your concerns regarding my level of experience?
> If 'Yes': Then let's … (introduce next step).
> If '*No*': Then what would set your mind at ease?

Client Objection

You have a number of competing listings in the market.

Don't REACT to it ...

An unskilled real estate agent would likely react using one of the following **JAWS** responses:

J ustify ... the circumstances:
> Agent: I never take on more than I can handle.

A ccuse ... the client, or third party, of a wrongdoing:
> (unlikely response)

W ithdraw ... from the relationship or situation:
> (unlikely response)

S arcasm ... directed toward the situation or individual:
> Agent: Thanks for noticing. Compliment accepted!

Defensive responses such as these will do nothing to alleviate the client's underlying concern. As a result, the client will likely disengage.

Client Objection

You have a number of competing listings in the market.

'ACRE' it!

A skilled agent would recognize this as a statement of mental stress and respond using the **ACRE** Formula©:

A lign ... by acknowledging, agreeing or empathizing:

Agent: It's true I currently have quite a few active listings!

C larify ... the underlying root cause of the stress:

Agent: Do you have a concern that there could be a conflict of interest?

> Client: *Yes! I feel your current listing inventory will take away from the showings on my property.*

R espond ... with evidence, an action plan or performance guarantee:

Agent: I understand your concern. Let me show you how my competing stock of inventory will actually increase the number of showings on your property ... (introduce evidence).

E ncourage ... the client to move forward:

Agent: Can you now see how my listing inventory will enhance your property's exposure?

> If 'Yes': Then let's ... (introduce next step).
> If '*No*': Then what would set your mind at ease?

Client Objection

You sound like everyone else.

Don't REACT to it ...

An unskilled real estate agent would likely react using one of the following **JAWS** responses:

J ustify ... the circumstances:

Agent: All commercial real estate companies provide essentially the same services.

A ccuse ... the client, or third party, of a wrongdoing:

(unlikely response)

W ithdraw ... from the relationship or situation:

(unlikely response)

S arcasm ... directed toward the situation or individual:

Agent: Impossible! We are without equal.

Defensive responses such as these will do nothing to alleviate the client's underlying concern. As a result, the client will likely disengage.

Client Objection

You sound like everyone else.

'ACRE' it!

A skilled agent would recognize this as a statement of mental stress and respond using the **ACRE** Formula©:

A lign ... by acknowledging, agreeing or empathizing:

Agent: I understand we might all seem similar on the surface.

C larify ... the underlying root cause of the stress:

Agent: What specific point of difference you are hoping to pin your listing decision on?
Client: *Something that demonstrates how my property will get broader exposure to prospective buyers.*

R espond ... with evidence, an action plan or performance guarantee:

Agent: Right then. Let me walk you through what we do to ensure your property gets exposed to a broader scope of prospective buyers than our competitors ... (introduce action plan).

E ncourage ... the client to move forward:

Agent: Can you see how that campaign will ensure your property will get a broader exposure to buyers?
If *'Yes'*: Then let's ... (introduce next step).
If *'No'*: Then what would it take to convince you?

Practice Using the ACRE Formula©
on mental stress

Activity: Consider the mentally stressed statement on the following page and create an **ACRE** Formula© response for it. Then check to see how your response compares to the author's response in the Appendix.

Client Objection

We have an existing relationship with one of your competitors.

Don't REACT to it ...

An unskilled real estate agent would likely react using one of the following **JAWS** responses:

J ustify ... the circumstances:

Agent: _____

A ccuse ... the client, or third party, of a wrongdoing:

Agent: _____

W ithdraw ... from the relationship or situation:

Agent: _____

S arcasm ... directed toward the situation or individual:

Agent: _____

Defensive responses such as these will do nothing to alleviate the client's underlying concern. As a result, the client will likely disengage.

Client Objection

We have an existing relationship with one of your competitors.

'ACRE' it!

A skilled agent would recognize this as a statement of mental stress and respond using the **ACRE** Formula©:

A lign ... by acknowledging, agreeing or empathizing:

Agent: _____

C larify ... the underlying root cause of the stress:

Agent: _____?
Client: _____
Agent: _____?
Client: _____

R espond ... with evidence, an action plan or performance guarantee:

Agent: _____
_____
_____

E ncourage ... the client to move forward:

Agent: _____
If 'Yes': Then I recommend we ... (next step).
If '*No*': Then what would set your mind at ease?

PART 2 - Emotional Stress

Accelerate successful client engagement experiences by recognizing and resolving your client's feelings of frustration, anxiety, resentment or hostility.

"Emotional stress is the condition that exists when a client experiences the emotions of frustration, resentment, or hostility during a negotiation."

Gerald G. Clerx

EMOTIONAL STRESS

When frustration, resentment, or hostility enters a negotiation, the transaction grinds to a halt. Momentum will not return until the *root cause* of that emotional state is uncovered and addressed.

Recognizing Emotional Stress

Like mental stress, emotional stress can be identified through what your client says during the engagement process.

Buyer/Tenant indicators:

- "I'm not happy with what you've shown me so far."

- "The sellers/landlords are being completely unrealistic!"

- "I don't like using brokers."

Seller/Landlord indicators:

- "This offer is insulting!"

- "It's taking a lot longer to lease than you said it would."

- "It would have been nice if your managing director showed up."

- "We had a bad experience with your company in the past."

The Difference Between Mental and Emotional Stress

While **mental stress** is rooted in *fear*, **emotional stress** is rooted in a *belief*—whether that belief is accurate or not.

- *"We had a bad experience with your company…"* → A belief that it might happen again.

- *"This offer is insulting!"* → Frustration from a belief that the offer undervalues the property.

- *"I don't like using agents!"* → Resentment from a belief that fees outweigh the value provided.

These beliefs—true or false—shape how the client interprets every word, gesture, and proposal you make.

Why Many Agents Make It Worse

When faced with an emotionally charged client, most agents respond instinctively rather than strategically. The result? They pour fuel on an already smoldering fire.

Your Role

In every negotiation, stay alert to statements that reveal emotional stress. When you hear them, resist the urge to react defensively.

Instead—**don't react to it… ACRE it!**

Statements of *Emotional* Stress

~ Buyer/Tenant ~

Client Objection

I'm not happy with what you've shown me to date!

Don't REACT to it ...

An unskilled real estate agent would likely react using one of the following **JAWS** responses:

J ustify ... the circumstances:
Agent: There is still a lot left to see.

A ccuse ... the client, or third party, of a wrongdoing:
Agent: Don't blame me ... supply is tight.

W ithdraw ... from the relationship or situation:
(unlikely response)

S arcasm ... directed toward the situation or individual:
Agent: That makes two of us.

Defensive responses such as these will do nothing to defuse the client's emotionally charged state. As a result, the client will likely disengage.

—

Client Objection

I'm not happy with what you've shown me to date!

'ACRE' it!

A skilled agent would recognize this as a statement of emotional stress and respond using the **ACRE** Formula©:

A lign ... by acknowledging, agreeing or empathizing:

Agent: I sensed your frustration.

C larify ... the underlying root cause of the stress:

Agent: Where are we missing the mark?
    Client: *Lots of viewings of unsuitable properties.*

R espond ... with an apology or explanation followed by a personal assurance or action plan:

Agent: Well that's on me … I apologize. Let's get together and narrow the search parameters down before looking at anything else.

E ncourage ... the client to move forward:

Agent: Do you have a few minutes to do that now?
    If *'Yes'*: Then let's talk about it.
    If *'No'*: Then when would be a better time?

Client Objection

The sellers/landlords are being completely unrealistic!

Don't REACT to it ...

An unskilled real estate agent would likely react using one of the following **JAWS** responses:

J ustify ... the circumstances:

Agent: That's normal given the state of the market.

A ccuse ... the client, or third party, of a wrongdoing:

(unlikely response)

W ithdraw ... from the relationship or situation:

Agent: You are under no obligation to pursue this property/space.

S arcasm ... directed toward the situation or individual:

Agent: Welcome to my world.

Defensive responses such as these will do nothing to defuse the client's emotionally charged state. As a result, the client will likely disengage.

Client Objection

The sellers/landlords are being completely unrealistic!

'ACRE' it!

A skilled agent would recognize this as a statement of emotional stress and respond using the **ACRE** Formula©:

A lign ... by acknowledging, agreeing or empathizing:

Agent: They do seem to feel quite confident about their property's value.

C larify ... the underlying root cause of the stress:

Agent: What do you feel a reasonable counter should have been?

> Client: *I think 'Y' dollars would have been more realistic.*

Agent: Is that what you feel represents fair value?

> Client: *Yes, somewhere around there.*

R espond ... with an apology or explanation followed by a personal assurance or action plan:

Agent: Their high expectations are likely a result of … (provide explanation). Here is what I recommend we do to find common ground … (introduce action plan).

E ncourage ... the client to move forward:

Agent: How does that sound?

> If *'Yes'*: Then leave it with me.
> If *'No'*: Then what would you suggest?

Client Objection

I don't like using brokers!

Don't REACT to it ...

An unskilled real estate agent would likely react using one of the following **JAWS** responses:

J ustify ... the circumstances:

Agent: You put yourself at risk by not engaging the services of a real estate agent.

A ccuse ... the client, or third party, of a wrongdoing:

(unlikely response)

W ithdraw ... from the relationship or situation:

(unlikely response)

S arcasm ... directed toward the situation or individual:

Agent: I don't like dentists but that's where I go when I need to fill a cavity.

Defensive responses such as these will do nothing to defuse the client's emotionally charged state. As a result, the client will likely disengage.

Client Objection

I don't like using brokers!

'ACRE' it!

A skilled agent would recognize this as a statement of emotional stress and respond using the **ACRE** Formula©:

A lign … by acknowledging, agreeing or empathizing:

    Agent: Not everyone does.

C larify … the underlying root cause of the stress:

    Agent: They usually have good reason. May I ask what yours is?
        Client: *No real added value!*
    Agent: Would you change your opinion if I could prove value?
        Client: *Perhaps.*

R espond … with an apology or explanation followed by a personal assurance or action plan:

    Agent: Let me walk you through how a good agent helps to mitigate risk and to broaden exposure to maximize results … (provide explanation).

E ncourage … the client to move forward:

    Agent: Does that adequately demonstrate the value we bring to a partnership?
        If *'Yes'*: Then let's … (introduce next step).
        If *'No'*: Then what would it take to convince you?

Statements of *Emotional* Stress

~ Seller/Landlord ~

Client Objection

This offer is insulting!

Don't REACT to it ...

An unskilled real estate agent would likely react using one of the following **JAWS** responses:

J ustify ... the circumstances:

  Agent: It's not that far out of line, given the market conditions.

A ccuse ... the client, or third party, of a wrongdoing:

  Agent: Well to be fair, your asking price is a little aggressive.

W ithdraw ... from the relationship or situation:

  Agent: You are under no obligation to respond.

S arcasm ... directed toward the situation or individual:

  Agent: Hey ... at least it's an offer!

Defensive responses such as these will do nothing to defuse the client's emotionally charged state. As a result, the client will likely disengage.

Client Objection

This offer is insulting!

'ACRE' it!

A skilled agent would recognize this as a statement of emotional stress and respond using the **ACRE** Formula©:

A lign ... by acknowledging, agreeing or empathizing:

Agent: I know it's less than what you were expecting.

C larify ... the underlying root cause of the stress:

Agent: Aside from the price is there anything else that you disagree with?

> Client: *No just the price really!*

R espond ... with an apology or explanation followed by a personal assurance or action plan:

Agent: Some buyers will start off with lowball offers even if they intend to come up to the full asking price. Here's what I recommend we do ... (introduce action plan).

E ncourage ... the client to move forward:

Agent: Does that seem like an appropriate way to respond?

> If *'Yes'*: I'll draw up the counter.
> If *'No'*: Then what would you recommend?

Client Objection

This is taking a lot longer to lease up than you said it would!

Don't REACT to it ...

An unskilled real estate agent would likely react using one of the following **JAWS** responses:

J ustify ... the circumstances:

Agent: Well, the market has softened considerably since I took over the project.

A ccuse ... the client, or third party, of a wrongdoing:

Agent: Well to be fair your delayed improvements did set us back a bit.

W ithdraw ... from the relationship or situation:

(unlikely response)

S arcasm ... directed toward the situation or individual:

Agent: Rome wasn't built in a day.

Defensive responses such as these will do nothing to defuse the client's emotionally charged state. As a result, the client will likely disengage.

Client Objection

This is taking a lot longer to lease up than you said it would!

'ACRE' it!

A skilled agent would recognize this as a statement of emotional stress and respond using the **ACRE** Formula©:

A lign ... by acknowledging, agreeing or empathizing:

Agent: Yes, it is! I share your frustration.

C larify ... the underlying root cause of the stress:

Agent: Is there anything specific you'd like to see done differently in our marketing efforts?
> Client: *I just need to see some tangible results!*

R espond ... with an apology or explanation followed by a personal assurance or action plan:

Agent: Here's the feedback I'm getting from the market (provide explanation). Here are some action steps I'll take immediately to stimulate additional interest in your property (introduce action plan).

E ncourage ... the client to move forward:

Agent: Does that seem to be a reasonable course of action?
> If *'Yes'*: Then leave it with me.
> If *'No'*: Then what would you like to see done?

Client Objection

It would have been nice if your MD were here!

Don't REACT to it ...

An unskilled real estate agent would likely react using one of the following **JAWS** responses:

J ustify ... the circumstances:

Agent: She was unfortunately tied up in other meetings.

A ccuse ... the client, or third party, of a wrongdoing:

(unlikely response)

W ithdraw ... from the relationship or situation:

(unlikely response)

S arcasm ... directed toward the situation or individual:

(unlikely response)

Defensive responses such as these will do nothing to defuse the client's emotionally charged state. As a result, the client will likely disengage.

Client Objection

It would have been nice if your MD were here!

'ACRE' it!

A skilled agent would recognize this as a statement of emotional stress and respond using the **ACRE** Formula©:

A lign ... by acknowledging, agreeing or empathizing:

Agent: I agree ... it would have been nice if she were able to attend!

C larify ... the underlying root cause of the stress:

Agent: Did you want her to be present in future meetings?

Client: *Not if she's too busy.*

R espond ... with an apology or explanation followed by a personal assurance or action plan:

Agent: I apologize that she was unable to attend this initial meeting. I will be sure to invite her to join us for all future meetings.

E ncourage ... the client to move forward:

Agent: How does that sound to you?

If *'Yes'*: Then consider it done.

If *'No'*: Would a phone call suffice in the interim?

Practice Using the ACRE Formula© on emotional stress

Activity: Consider the emotionally stressed statement on the following page and create an **ACRE** Formula© response for it. Then check to see how your response compares to the author's response in the Appendix.

Client Objection

We had a bad experience with your company in the past!

Don't REACT to it ...

An unskilled real estate agent would likely react using one of the following **JAWS** responses:

J ustify ... the circumstances:

Agent: _____

A ccuse ... the client, or third party, of a wrongdoing:

Agent: _____

W ithdraw ... from the relationship or situation:

Agent: _____

S arcasm ... directed toward the situation or individual:

Agent: _____

Defensive responses such as these will do nothing to defuse the client's emotionally charged state. As a result, the client will likely disengage.

Client Objection

We had a bad experience with your company in the past!

'ACRE' It!

A skilled agent would recognize this as a statement of emotional stress and respond using the **ACRE** Formula©:

A lign ... by acknowledging, agreeing or empathizing:

Agent: _____

C larify ... the underlying root cause of the stress:

Agent: _____?
    Client: _____

Agent: _____?
    Client: _____

R espond ... with an apology or explanation followed by a personal assurance or action plan:

Agent: _____

_____.

E ncourage ... the client to move forward:

Agent: _____

    If *'Yes'*: Then I recommend we ... (next step).
    If *'No'*: Then what would you recommend?

PART 3 - Positional Stress

Accelerate successful client engagement experiences by recognizing and resolving positional impasses.

"Position stress is the condition that exists when both parties of a negotiation become positional regarding the price, dates, terms, or conditions of the agreement."

Gerald G. Clerx

POSITIONAL STRESS

When **positional stress** enters a negotiation, progress stalls and will not resume until the client's **underlying interests** are uncovered and a solution is crafted that both sides can accept.

Recognizing Positional Stress

Verbally, positional stress is usually easy to spot. Listen for inflexible language such as *"I must have," "I will not,"* or *"I refuse to"* — clear signals your client is locked into a stance.
In commercial real estate, these positions often involve **timelines, price, deposits, terms and conditions,** or **tenant improvement (TI) allowances**.

Buyer/Tenant statements may include:

- "What fee rebates are you prepared to offer us?"

- "I'll take it if the landlord adds two more months free rent."

- "Tell them to take it or leave it. That's my final offer."

- "I need another week for subject removal."

Seller/Landlord statements may include:

- "I want a cancellation agreement."

- "We require a few exclusions to the listing/leasing agreement."

- "I'll give you the business if you reduce your fee by 20%."

- "I refuse to pay a full commission on such an easy deal."

- "Can you guarantee your results?"

Uncovering the Real Interest

The most effective way to move past a rigid position is to explore *why* it matters to your client. Use clarifying questions such as:

- "Why is that important to you?"

- "What are you basing that on?"

- "What specific concerns do you have?"

- "What do you hope to achieve by that?"

- "Help me understand your objective."

Responding to Positional Stress

When faced with a forceful position, the instinct is to counter with one of your own. **Resist this urge.** Meeting force with force pushes both parties deeper into their stances, making compromise less likely.
Instead, maintain composure and approach the situation non-defensively. This opens the door to a constructive exchange where interests — rather than positions — drive the solution.

In the next section, we'll explore how to apply the **ACRE Formula©** to defuse positional stress and move negotiations forward.

Statements of *Positional* Stress
~ Buyer/Tenant ~

Client Objection

What fee rebates are you prepared to offer us?

Don't REACT to it ...

An unskilled real estate agent would likely react using one of the following **JAWS** responses:

J ustify ... the circumstances:

Agent: It is not our policy to give out fee rebates.

A ccuse ... the client, or third party, of a wrongdoing:

(unlikely response)

W ithdraw ... from the relationship or situation:

Agent: I'm not prepared to do that.

S arcasm ... directed toward the situation or individual:

(unlikely response)

Defensive responses such as these will do nothing to satisfy the client's underlying interest. As a result, the client will likely disengage.

Client Objection

What fee rebates are you prepared to offer us?

'ACRE' it!

A skilled agent would recognize this as a statement of positional stress and respond using the **ACRE** Formula©:

A lign ... by acknowledging, agreeing or empathizing:

Agent: I'm open to having that conversation.

C larify ... the underlying root cause of the stress:

Agent: What rebate amount are you seeking to obtain?
Client: *I think $20,000 is reasonable.*

Agent: Why $20,000?
Client: *Because that is what our last agent gave us.*

R espond ... with an interest-based proposal:

Agent: Here's what I suggest we do. Let's revisit this conversation once we have a deal on the table. If at that time you feel a fee rebate is justified, then I'm happy to pick up where we left off.

E ncourage ... the client to move forward:

Agent: How does that sound?
If *'Yes'*: Great!
If *'No'*: Then what would you like to propose?

Client Objection

I'll take it as long as the landlord agrees to throw in an additional two months of free rent.

Don't REACT to it ...

An unskilled real estate agent would likely react using one of the following **JAWS** responses:

J ustify ... the circumstances:

Agent: You are already getting a good deal as it is!

A ccuse ... the client, or third party, of a wrongdoing:

Agent: That's an unreasonable request.

W ithdraw ... from the relationship or situation:

(unlikely response)

S arcasm ... directed toward the situation or individual:

(unlikely response)

Defensive responses such as these will do nothing to satisfy the client's underlying interest. As a result, the client will likely disengage.

Client Objection

I'll take it as long as the landlord agrees to throw in an additional two months of free rent.

'ACRE' it!

A skilled agent would recognize this as a statement of positional stress and respond using the **ACRE** Formula©:

A lign ... by acknowledging, agreeing or empathizing:

> Agent: I'll do what I can to make this deal work for you.

C larify ... the underlying root cause of the stress:

> Agent: Why do you feel it's a reasonable request to ask for two additional months free rent at this late stage?
> > Client: *Because I think I can get it!*

> Agent: Is this a deal-breaker if he says 'no'?
> > Client: *No ... but there is no harm asking!*

R espond ... with an interest-based proposal:

> Agent: Here's what I recommend we do. I will talk to the landlord about the additional free rent and see if he's amenable. If not, I suggest we offer up an exchange concession as a show of good faith.

E ncourage ... the client to move forward:

> Agent: How does that sound?
> > If *'Yes'*: Leave it with me,
> > If *'No'*: Then what would you propose?

Client Objection

Tell them they can take it or leave it … that's my final offer.

Don't REACT to it …

An unskilled real estate agent would likely react using one of the following **JAWS** responses:

J ustify … the circumstances:

Agent: Threats of finality are rarely a good idea in a negotiation.

A ccuse … the client, or third party, of a wrongdoing:

Agent: A bit harsh don't you think.

W ithdraw … from the relationship or situation:

(unlikely response)

S arcasm … directed toward the situation or individual:

(unlikely response)

Defensive responses such as these will do nothing to satisfy the client's underlying interest. As a result, the client will likely disengage.

Client Objection

Tell them they can take it or leave it ... that's my final offer.

'ACRE' it!

A skilled agent would recognize this as a statement of positional stress and respond using the **ACRE** Formula©:

A lign ... by acknowledging, agreeing or empathizing:

Agent: I can appreciate that you want to achieve the best deal possible.

C larify ... the underlying root cause of the stress:

Agent: May I ask why you believe 'X' dollars is a fair 'final offer' price?
> Client: *Because that's all I'm willing to spend on this.*

Agent: Do you have flexibility elsewhere regarding dates, terms or conditions?
> Client: *I can bend a little bit on the completion date.*

R espond ... with an interest-based proposal:

Agent: Well in that case I recommend we offer up an earlier completion date in exchange for a price concession, since that would benefit the owner.

E ncourage ... the client to move forward:

Agent: Does that seem like a reasonable trade-off?
> If *'Yes'*: I'll draft it up.
> If *'No'*: Then what would you propose?

Client Objection

I need another week for subject removal.

Don't REACT to it ...

An unskilled real estate agent would likely react using one of the following **JAWS** responses:

J ustify ... the circumstances:

Agent: I can't imagine the seller agreeing to that.

A ccuse ... the client, or third party, of a wrongdoing:

Agent: That's an unreasonable request to make.

W ithdraw ... from the relationship or situation:

(unlikely response)

S arcasm ... directed toward the situation or individual:

(unlikely response)

Defensive responses such as these will do nothing to satisfy the client's underlying interest. As a result, the client will likely disengage.

Client Objection

I need another week for subject removal.

'ACRE' it!

A skilled agent would recognize this as a statement of positional stress and respond using the **ACRE** Formula©:

A lign ... by acknowledging, agreeing or empathizing:

Agent: Understood!

C larify ... the underlying root cause of the stress:

Agent: May I ask why?
  Client: *I want to explore some other financing options.*

Agent: Do you need the full week?
  Client: *I might be able to tighten the timelines a bit.*

R espond ... with an interest-based proposal:

Agent: Here's what I suggest we do. I don't think it's reasonable to ask my client for another full week, however I do think they might consider another 2 days to explore your financing options.

E ncourage ... the client to move forward:

Agent: Can you make that timeline work?
  If *'Yes'*: Leave it with me.
  If *'No'*: Then what reduced time frame could you make work?

Statements of *Positional* Stress

~ Seller/Landlord ~

Client Objection

I'd like a cancellation agreement.

Don't REACT to it ...

An unskilled real estate agent would likely react using one of the following **JAWS** responses:

J ustify ... the circumstances:

Agent: We've never had a client feel the need to cancel an agreement with us.

A ccuse ... the client, or third party, of a wrongdoing:

(unlikely response)

W ithdraw ... from the relationship or situation:

Agent: Sorry, I'm unwilling to do that!

S arcasm ... directed toward the situation or individual:

Agent: You sound like my ex-wife.

Defensive responses such as these will do nothing to satisfy the client's underlying interest. As a result, the client will likely disengage.

Client Objection

I'd like a cancellation agreement.

'ACRE' it!

A skilled agent would recognize this as a statement of positional stress and respond using the **ACRE** Formula©:

A lign ... by acknowledging, agreeing or empathizing:

Agent: Let's talk about that.

Clarify ... the underlying root cause of the stress:

Agent: May I ask why a cancellation agreement is important to you?

>   Client: *If I'm not happy with your work I want the right to cancel my listing.*

R espond ... with an interest-based proposal:

Agent: Here's what I would be willing to do. I'll provide you with the right to cancel, under specific circumstances … (introduce conditions).

E ncourage ... the client to move forward:

Agent: Would that be agreeable to you?
>   If *'Yes'*: I'll draft it up.
>   If *'No'*: Then what would you propose?

Client Objection

We will require a few exclusions to the listing/leasing agreement.

Don't REACT to it ...

An unskilled real estate agent would likely react using one of the following **JAWS** responses:

J ustify ... the circumstances:

Agent: You will achieve a far better outcome if you give us full control of the selling/leasing process.

A ccuse ... the client, or third party, of a wrongdoing:

(unlikely response)

W ithdraw ... from the relationship or situation:

Agent: Sorry, that's not something I'm prepared to do!

S arcasm ... directed toward the situation or individual:

(unlikely response)

Defensive responses such as these will do nothing to satisfy the client's underlying interest. As a result, the client will likely disengage.

Client Objection

We will require a few exclusions to the listing/leasing agreement.

'ACRE' it!

A skilled agent would recognize this as a statement of positional stress and respond using the **ACRE** Formula©:

A lign ... by acknowledging, agreeing or empathizing:

Agent: I'm prepared to consider it.

C larify ... the underlying root cause of the stress:

Agent: Who do you want excluded from the agreement?

> Client: *Two companies ('X' and 'Y') have approached us privately. We'd like them excluded.*

Agent: How far have your conversations gone with these two companies?

> Client: *At this point they've just expressed an interest.*

R espond ... with an interest-based proposal:

Agent: Before you meet with these two companies, I'd like to expose your property to the broader market to encourage competition. If you decide to sell/lease to either 'X' or 'Y' company, I'll reduce my fee by 30%.

E ncourage ... the client to move forward:

Agent: Does that seem reasonable?

> If '*Yes*': Consider it done.
> If '*No*': Then what would you propose?

Client Objection

I'm prepared to give you the business if you'd reduce your fee by 20%.

Don't REACT to it ...

An unskilled real estate agent would likely react using one of the following **JAWS** responses:

J ustify ... the circumstances:

Agent: I'm not sure it's a prudent decision to award your business to someone willing to discount their fees!

A ccuse ... the client, or third party, of a wrongdoing:

(unlikely response)

W ithdraw ... from the relationship or situation:

Agent: That's not something I'm prepared to do!

S arcasm ... directed toward the situation or individual:

Agent: Sure, assuming you are prepared to reduce your expectations by 20%.

Defensive responses such as these will do nothing to satisfy the client's underlying interest. As a result, the client will likely disengage.

Client Objection

I'm prepared to give you the business if you'd reduce your fee by 20%.

'ACRE' it!

A skilled agent would recognize this as a statement of positional stress and respond using the **ACRE** Formula©:

A lign ... by acknowledging, agreeing or empathizing:

Agent: Well, let's talk about that.

C larify ... the underlying root cause of the stress:

Agent: First off ... why 20%?

> Client: *I've got a lot of other companies vying for my business. I'm prepared to offer it to you if you'll accept the same fee as your closest competitor.*

R espond ... with an interest-based proposal:

Agent: Then here's what I suggest we do. I'll reduce my fees by 20% for any deals below 'x' dollars assuming you'll kick in a 20% bonus for any results we achieve above that amount.

E ncourage ... the client to move forward:

Agent: Does that seem like a fair compromise?

> If *'Yes'*: Then I'll draft it up.
>
> If *'No'*: Then what would you like to propose?

Client Objection

I refuse to pay a full commission on such an easy transaction.

Don't REACT to it ...

An unskilled real estate agent would likely react using one of the following **JAWS** responses:

J ustify ... the circumstances:

> Agent: I can assure you this was far from 'an easy transaction'.

A ccuse ... the client, or third party, of a wrongdoing:

> (unlikely response)

W ithdraw ... from the relationship or situation:

> (unlikely response)

S arcasm ... directed toward the situation or individual:

> Agent: Our listing agreement states otherwise.

Defensive responses such as these will do nothing to satisfy the client's underlying interest. As a result, the client will likely disengage.

Client Objection

I refuse to pay a full commission on such an easy transaction.

'ACRE' it!

A skilled agent would recognize this as a statement of positional stress and respond using the **ACRE** Formula©:

A lign ... by acknowledging, agreeing or empathizing:

Agent: It's important to me that you feel my FULL fees are warranted!

C larify ... the underlying root cause of the stress:

Agent: When you say, 'an easy transaction' can I ask what you are referencing?
    Client: *$80,000 is a lot of money for a few weeks work!*

Agent: Are you evaluating my fee on 'time invested' or 'outcome achieved'?
    Client: *'Time invested' I guess.*

R espond ... with an interest-based proposal:

Agent: Given that it is the 'outcome achieved' that determines my compensation I don't feel it would be warranted to reduce my fees. I would, however, be prepared to (offer alternate concession).

E ncourage ... the client to move forward:

Agent: How does that sound?
    If *'Yes'*: Then let's ... (introduce next step).
    If *'No'*: Then what would seem reasonable to you?

Practice Using the ACRE Formula©
on positional stress

Activity: Consider the positionally stressed statement on the following page and create an **ACRE** Formula© response for it. Then check to see how your response compared to the author's response in the Appendix.

Client Objection

Are you prepared to guarantee your results?

Don't REACT to it ...

An unskilled real estate agent would likely react using one of the following **JAWS** responses:

J ustify ... the circumstances:

    Agent: _____

A ccuse ... the client, or third party, of a wrongdoing:

    Agent: _____

W ithdraw ... from the relationship or situation:

    Agent: _____

S arcasm ... directed toward the situation or individual:

    Agent: _____

Defensive responses such as these will do nothing to satisfy the client's underlying interest. As a result, the client will likely disengage.

Client Objection

Are you prepared to guarantee your results?

'ACRE' It!

A skilled agent would recognize this as a statement of positional stress and respond using the **ACRE** Formula©:

A lign ... by acknowledging, agreeing or empathizing:

Agent: _____

C larify ... the underlying root cause of the stress:

Agent: _____?
Client: _____
Agent: _____?
Client: _____

R espond ... with an interest-based proposal:

Agent: _____
_____

E ncourage ... the client to move forward:

Agent: _____
If *'Yes'*: Then I recommend we ... (next step).
If *'No'*: Then what would you propose?

Summary

As an experienced real estate agent, you know negotiating stress is simply part of the job. Every client brings fears, emotions, and limits. A completely stress-free transaction? About as rare as a rainy day in Southern California — possible, but unlikely.

Stress is the constant in every deal. How *you* respond is the variable that sets you apart. Agents who master the art of resolving **mental, emotional, and positional stress** are in high demand — and short supply.

The **ACRE Formula©** is your proven strategy for overcoming client fear, managing emotions, and resolving entrenched positions.

When you respond skillfully to these three deal breakers, you take control of the negotiation, boost your chances of closing, and create loyal, satisfied clients.

From this moment forward, whenever client stress arises, remember this:
Don't REACT to it... 'ACRE' it!

Engage BRILLIANTLY!

Gerald G. Clerx
Accelerating Client Engagement

APPENDIX

Client Objection

We have an existing relationship with one of your competitors.

Don't REACT to it ...

An unskilled real estate agent would likely react using one of the following **JAWS** responses:

J ustify ... the circumstances:

Agent: But we are the dominant team in the market and can offer you far more than they can.

A ccuse ... the client, or third party, of a wrongdoing:

(unlikely response)

W ithdraw ... from the relationship or situation:

(unlikely response)

S arcasm ... directed toward the situation or individual:

Agent: I didn't know we had any real competitors.

Defensive responses such as these will do nothing to alleviate the client's underlying concern. As a result, the client will likely disengage.

Client Objection

We have an existing relationship with one of your competitors.

'ACRE' it!

A skilled agent would recognize this as a statement of mental stress and respond using the **ACRE** Formula©:

A lign ... by acknowledging, agreeing or empathizing:

Agent: Good relationships ARE important in this business!

C larify ... the underlying root cause of the stress:

Agent: Have you considered the advantages of expanding your corporate partnerships?
Client: *What advantages are you talking about?*

R espond ... with evidence, an action plan or performance guarantee:

Agent: Our clients tell us there are three unique advantages we bring to our clients that our competitors do not ... (introduce evidence).

E ncourage ... the client to move forward:

Agent: Would these unique services be an asset to your organization as well?
If *'Yes'*: Then let's ... (next step).
If *'No'*: Then what would compel you to invest in a relationship with us?

Client Objection

We had a bad experience with one of your real estate agents and don't plan on using your company again!

Don't REACT to it ...

An unskilled real estate agent would likely react using one of the following **JAWS** responses:

J ustify ... the circumstances:

Agent: Yes, but the experience wasn't with me.

A ccuse ... the client, or third party, of a wrongdoing:

(unlikely response)

W ithdraw ... from the relationship or situation:

(unlikely response)

S arcasm ... directed toward the situation or individual:

Agent: Whoever it was no longer works for us!

Defensive responses such as these will do nothing to neutralize the client's emotionally charged state. As a result, the client will likely disengage.

Client Objection

We had a bad experience with one of your real estate agents and don't plan on using your company again!

'ACRE' it!

A skilled agent would recognize this as a statement of emotional stress and respond using the **ACRE** Formula©:

A lign ... by acknowledging, agreeing or empathizing:

Agent: I am sorry to hear that!

C larify ... the underlying root cause of the stress:

Agent: In a nutshell can you tell me what happened!
Client: *A simple case of overpromising and under-delivering.*

R espond ... with an apology, an explanation or personal assurance:

Agent: I'm sorry you've had a bad experience with us. That should not have happened. I'd like to extend you my personal assurance that you will be fully satisfied with our service standards moving forward.

E ncourage ... the client to move forward:

Agent: Would you be willing to give our company a chance to redeem ourselves?
If *'Yes'*: Then let's ... (introduce next step).
If *'No'*: Then what would it take to earn back your business?

Client Objection

Are you prepared to guarantee your results?

Don't REACT to it ...

An unskilled real estate agent would likely react using one of the following **JAWS** responses:

J ustify ... the circumstances:

Agent: There are too many variables involved for me to feel comfortable about offering you a guarantee!

A ccuse ... the client, or third party, of a wrongdoing:

(unlikely response)

W ithdraw ... from the relationship or situation:

Agent: I'm not prepared to do that!

S arcasm ... directed toward the situation or individual:

(unlikely response)

Defensive responses such as these will do nothing to satisfy the client's underlying interest. As a result, the client will likely disengage.

Client Objection

Are you prepared to guarantee your results?

'ACRE' it!

A skilled agent would recognize this as a statement of positional stress and respond using the **ACRE** Formula©:

A lign ... by acknowledging, agreeing or empathizing:

Agent: I would consider it!

C larify ... the underlying root cause of the stress:

Agent: What guarantees are you after?
Client: *If you don't produce the result you've promised, I don't pay you.*

R espond ... with an interest-based proposal:

Agent: I'm not prepared to go that far, however, I am prepared to enter into a performance-based agreement in which compensation is tied to specific KPI's.

E ncourage ... the client to move forward:

Agent: How does that sound?
If *'Yes'*: Then let's ... (introduce next step).
If *'No'*: Then what would you like to propose?

About the Author

When it comes to **Client Engagement**, Gerald Gordon Clerx is recognized worldwide as a leading authority.

Gerald is the author of *Engage BRILLIANTLY* and the creator of both the **GAP Analysis Client Engagement Model**© and the **ACRE Formula**© — tools designed to transform how real estate professionals connect with clients.

His service promise is clear: equip clients with the skills, insights, and resources to **double their business win rate** while simultaneously **raising customer satisfaction**.

Over the past 15 years, Gerald has delivered on that promise globally, training and coaching commercial real estate agents across 28 countries to excel at assessing client needs, presenting client-focused solutions, and negotiating collaborative deals.

One of the world's top real estate services firms relies on Gerald's GAP Analysis Model© and ACRE Formula© to help successfully transact over **$160 billion** in commercial real estate every year.

SPEAKING ENGAGEMENTS

Gerald Gordon Clerx has been called the 'Client Engagement Guru' who truly practices what he preaches.

He is a masterful presenter. His *engaging, entertaining*, and *inspiring* presentation style make him one of most sought-after speakers in his profession. The skill sets and tools he imparts are powerful, practical and, most importantly, immediately applicable.

To have Gerald Gordon Clerx speak at your next conference, email Jaydyn@GeraldClerx.com.

Praise from course participants

"When it comes to training in sales and negotiation, there is simply no one better than Gerald Clerx. Gerald has trained my brokers on several occasions both here in the USA and abroad and the results are profound and measurable. In addition to the skills transfer in his courses, they are high energy, interactive, and above all...fun. It is with pleasure that I recommend Gerald to any organization looking to improve the skills of their people."
David P. – Office Manager | Los Angeles, USA

"Gerald's training series was an eye-opener and truly an inspirational experience for me. I have had the privilege to not only take part in 'BRIDGING the GAP' but also be able to witness the impact of Gerald's work over all employees of my company, sales and non-sales, who continue to benefit from this concept daily. The concept and the way Gerald delivers it to graduates is one of the most influential tools I have ever experienced in my industry."
Iglika Y. – Office Manager | Sofia, Bulgaria

"I recently undertook 'BRIDGING the GAP' training series with Gerald Clerx over three days. It was the best single training session that I have ever attended and changed the way that I perform in my work environment for the better. Consequently, I am achieving results at work that I didn't think were possible. I would highly recommend undertaking the 'BRIDGING the GAP' training series if ever given the opportunity."

Stephanie T. – Agent | Melbourne, Australia

"I have completed several courses with Gerald over the past 6 or 7 years and I can honestly admit I use the skills and techniques that he promotes in my business on a daily basis, as do many of my colleagues who have attended similar courses with Gerald. In preparing each pitch to win an appointment I continually find myself referring back to Gerald's advice; looking to both read my target and align my offering with what they are trying to achieve. I have found these strategies to be highly effective, winning us countless jobs that seemed unobtainable prior to our winning pitch."

Anthony W. - Director of Sales - Brisbane, Australia

"Gerald is a fantastic presenter whose teachings have helped me excel not only in the workplace but also in my personal life. I look forward to taking Gerald's course for years to come."

Ted M. - Agent | Vancouver, Canada

"I had the privilege to hear Gerald speak on presentation skills and the use of personality profiling to maximize sales presentation results. I was overly impressed with his style of communication and his ability to engage me in to his topic. I wish we could have had more time with Gerald to learn even more. However, I was surprised by how much I took away from his presentation in only a short amount of time. Gerald has given me techniques to implement that have changed my business tenfold!"

Melissa M. – Office Manager | Reno, USA

"Gerald's 'BRIDGING the GAP' training sessions are the best I have encountered to date, as far as content and delivery are concerned. It was in fact the only sessions I have attended that accurately address the common issues professionals face accompanied by appropriate strategies to address them moving forward. The interactive components of this course were second to none. I currently use several of the techniques taught by Gerald on an ongoing basis and would have no hesitation in recommending Gerald and his 'BRIDGING the GAP' training exercises."

Marcel E. - Agent | Sydney, Australia

"Gerald's perspective on understanding the personalities of prospects that you may be presenting to, and his strategy for delivering a message, or "value proposition", has greatly improved my success rate in competitive pitches. Gerald's 'BRIDGING the GAP' structure has also helped me to guide discussions in meetings, and provide verbal answers to "on the spot" questions in a way that resonates with my clients and prospects. I would recommend Gerald Clerx training over any other sales training that I have had in 12 years of working as a sales representative for multi-national corporations."

Alan D. - Agent | Ottawa, Canada

"I attended a number of 'BRIDGING the GAP' training session which Gerald facilitated. Anyone who wants to improve their skill set in obtaining a better understanding on who their clients are, what they want and how to move them from their current reality to their desired reality, should make these training sessions a priority!!!"

Paul F. - Agent | Sydney, Australia

"Gerald is an articulate, succinct, and inspired instructor who has broadened my knowledge and understanding of assessment, presentation, and negotiations. I have taken a number of courses from Gerald both on-line and in person. I consider all of them valuable learning experiences."

John L. - Agent | Toronto, Canada

"I have undertaken numerous courses conducted by Gerald Clerx. The course relating to engagement styles profiling was very interesting and Gerald was able to provide real life examples of how this has worked for him. This course was informative and I was able to take away tools that I could use not only at work but also in my personal life. Gerald's style of coaching/ training is second to none. He is interactive with the class, humorous and likeable. I have no hesitation in recommending Gerald as a trainer and I will continue to undertake his courses throughout my career."

Amanda A. - Agent | Melbourne, Australia

"Gerald's 'BRIDGING the GAP' seminar is an excellent tool for Success partners. It opened my eyes to how I was running my business currently and what I needed to implement into my day-to-day business to get the results I am looking for. A very worthwhile experience!"

Adam K. - Agent | Toronto Canada

"This was my second course with Gerald and I have to say that he has a unique ability to transfer the knowledge and experience, enough to positively energize all of the people he comes in contact with. Although extremely technically minded Gerald has the ability to communicate with simple, friendly language with a great sense of humor."

Kreso R. - Agent | Zagreb, Croatia

"In 18 years in the industry I have participated in numerous training courses and workshops. The two courses of Gerald's that I have participated in have been in have been amongst the most memorable. Very relevant content and great delivery. I look forward to the next one."

Simon K. – Office Manager | Wollongong, Australia

"I have had the privilege of being trained by Gerald on several different courses, these training sessions have all been entertaining, informative and most of all productive which has resulted in my career accelerating to new levels. In recent times I have found the formulas taught through the courses to be invaluable in setting me apart from my competitors and allowing me to continue to grow my business and brand in a tighter market. I have no hesitation in recommending any of Gerald's courses to anyone!"

Paul T. - Agent | Adelaide, Australia

"Gerald is a difference maker! His 'BRIDGING the GAP' workshop was incredibly helpful and will be the driver behind our office winning more pitches."

Yumi P. - Agent | Indiana, USA

"If you get the chance to participate in any of Gerald's courses I would highly recommend the opportunity. I recently participated in Gerald's 'BRIDGING the GAP' seminar for a second time and highly recommended anyone whose business is client driven to participate in this course. Gerald's presentation skills keep the group fully active and engaged in the entire days program which is hard to do with a large group, over a extended period of time."

Matt S. - Agent | Vancouver, Canada

"Gerald's 'BRIDGING the GAP' training was probably one of the most memorable that I have attended, not only because Gerald is very talented presenter who connects with the audience in an instant, moreover because the course has changed my ability to win deals and gain partners forever."

Verka P. – Office Manager | Sofia, Bulgaria